W9-DCB-833

Raising the Bar:

A Lawyer's Book of Quotes

Raising the Bar:
A Lawyer's Book of Quotes

Edited by Carol Kelly-Gangi

**BARNES
& NOBLE
BOOKS**
NEW YORK

For Dad with love and gratitude.

A special thanks to my sister, Barbara Kelly-Vergona,
for her valuable assistance, helpful suggestions, and support.

The quotes in this book have been drawn from many
sources, and are assumed to be accurate as quoted in their
previously published forms. Although every effort has been
made to verify the quotes and sources, the publisher
cannot guarantee their perfect accuracy.

2004 Barnes & Noble Books

ISBN 0-7607-4887-X

Printed and bound in the United States of America

04 05 06 07 HC 9 8 7 6 5 4 3 2 1

FEW PROFESSIONS ELICIT THE IRE AND CONTEMPT OF
the general public as does the practice of law. Sure,
when we find ourselves in need of a lawyer, we want
the best that our means can afford. If the matter
is litigation, we hope our attorney will vigorously
advocate for us all the way to the Supreme Court if
necessary. So why do we love to hate them so much?
Granted, the field has its fair share of sharks, shysters,
and ambulance chasers. But some of the most prin-
cipled and hardworking people you'll ever meet are
also in the profession. In fact, many of the people
most admired in history were drawn to the practice
of law at one time or another in their lives.

    Raising the Bar: A Lawyer's Book of Quotes is a
collection of quotations for and about lawyers and
the legal profession. It contains hundreds of quotes
from lawyers and non-lawyers alike about this age-
old vocation. Contributors as diverse as F. Lee Bailey,
Cicero, Hillary Rodham Clinton, Albert Einstein,
Thomas Jefferson, Martin Luther King, Jr., and

Mark Twain offer selections that ebb and flow like a lively debate on the subjects of justice, the practice of law, and the lawyer's role in society. And as if they are advocating from opposing sides, many of the speakers come to opposite conclusions about precisely the same issue. You'll read firsthand accounts of the rigors of law school from the likes of Abraham Lincoln and Oliver Wendell Holmes, as well as proverbs and maxims, and tips of the trade from renowned lawyers. And what legal quote book would be complete without a dose of lawyer jokes?

Whether you're a top-notch litigator, a public interest lawyer, or simply in love with the law, it is hoped that *Raising the Bar* will help to shed some new light on this often-berated but noble profession.

–Carol Kelly-Gangi
Rumson, NJ 2004

On Lawyers...

Most good lawyers live well, work hard, and die poor.

     —DANIEL WEBSTER, lawyer and statesman

A reputable lawyer will advise you to keep out of the law, make the best of a foolish bargain, and not get caught again.

     —MARK TWAIN, humorist and writer

The mere title of lawyer is sufficient to deprive a man of the public confidence.... The most innocent and irreproachable life cannot guard a lawyer against the hatred of his fellow citizens.

—JOHN QUINCY ADAMS,
6th president of the United States

What the lawyer needs to redeem himself is not more ability, but more courage in the face of financial loss and personal ill will to stand for right and justice.

—LOUIS D. BRANDEIS, Supreme Court Justice

Being a lawyer is about serving justice. That's not only our greatest calling, it's our only calling.

—ELLIS RUBIN, lawyer

Lawyers as a group are no more dedicated to justice or public service than a private utility is dedicated to giving light.

—DAVID MELINKOFF, professor

I have a high opinion of lawyers. With all their faults, they stack up well against those in every other occupation or profession. They are better to work with or play with or fight with or drink with than most other varieties of mankind.

—HARRISON TWEED, lawyer

I don't know of any other industry, except the movie business, that has so many stars. Every lawyer thinks he's special.

—PETER MORRISON, entertainer and lawyer

Lawyers are like rhinoceroses: thick-skinned, short-sighed, and always ready to charge.

—DAVID MELLOR, British political leader

I've never met a litigator who didn't think he was winning—right up until the moment the guillotine dropped.

—WILLIAM F. BAXTER,
assistant U.S. attorney general

I get paid for seeing that my clients have every break the law allows. I have knowingly defended a number of guilty men. But the guilty never escaped unscathed. My fees are sufficient punishment for anyone.

—F. LEE BAILEY, lawyer

A lawyer's time and advice are his stock in trade.

—Attributed to ABRAHAM LINCOLN

I always felt from the beginning that you had to defend people you disliked and feared as well as those you admired.

—ROGER BALDWIN, reformer

Honest criminal defense lawyers will tell you that they live in terror of innocent clients, if only because the overwhelming majority of criminal cases end in a conviction of one sort or another.

—JOHNNIE L. COCHRAN, JR., from *Journey To Justice*

The negative interpretation of the legal mind sees the lawyer as focusing excessively on rules and details, and disregarding the broader considerations of humanity or social policy.... The key traits of the legal mind in its most positive senses are the able lawyer's ability to analyze events, to develop facts and separate fancy, and to assign governing rules or consequences to the facts. Here is the heart of the professional lawyer's talent: the ability to think through to the central issue, to the core of the matter.

—BERTRAM HARNETT from *Law, Lawyers, and Laymen*

Lawyers use the law as shoemakers use leather: rubbing it, pressing it, and stretching it with their teeth, all to the end of making it fit for their purposes.

—LOUIS XII, King of France

No poet ever interpreted nature as freely as a lawyer interprets the truth.

—JEAN GIRAUDOUX, writer

A society of men bred up from their youth in the art of proving by words multiplied for the purpose that white is black and black is white according as they are paid.

—JONATHAN SWIFT, cleric and writer

Lawyers like to throw around jargon and flowery language because it makes them feel self-important and prestigious.

—GEORGE HATHAWAY, writer

Come, you of the law, who can talk, if you please,
Till the man in the moon will allow it's a cheese.

—OLIVER WENDELL HOLMES, SR.,
physician, professor, and writer

Most lawyers who win a case advise their clients
that "we have won" and, when justice has frowned
upon their cause, that "you have lost."

—LOUIS NIZER, lawyer and writer

Deals aren't usually blown by principals; they're
blown by lawyers and accountants trying to prove
how valuable they are.

—ROBERT TOWNSEND, professor

A well-known occupational hazard of lawyers is their tendency to become contentious, and to develop such associated traits as being arrogant, deceitful, and punitive.

—DAVID RILEY, lawyer and writer

Lawyers spend a great deal of their time shoveling smoke.

—OLIVER WENDELL HOLMES, JR.,
Supreme Court Justice

He is no lawyer who cannot take two sides.

—CHARLES LAMB, essayist and critic

Lawyers are the only persons in whom ignorance of the law is not punished.

—JEREMY BENTHAM, jurist and philosopher

An incompetent lawyer can delay a trial for months or years. A competent lawyer can delay one even longer.

—EVELLE YOUNGER, lawyer

It isn't the bad lawyers who are screwing up the justice system in this country—it's the good lawyers. If you have two competent lawyers on opposite sides, a trial that should take three days could easily last six months.

—ART BUCHWALD, humorist and writer

Young lawyers attend the courts, not because they have business there but because they have no business anywhere else.

—WASHINGTON IRVING, writer

Lawyers with a weakness for seeing the merits of the other side end up being employed by neither.

—RICHARD J. BARNET from *Roots of War*

They have no lawyers among them [in Utopia] for they consider them as the sort of people whose profession it is to disguise matters.

—THOMAS MORE from *Utopia*

How many times I have laughed at your telling me plainly that I was too lazy to be anything but a lawyer.

—ABRAHAM LINCOLN,
16th president of the United States

Three Philadelphia lawyers are a match for the Devil.

—POPULAR SAYING, early 19th century

My daddy is a movie actor, and sometimes he plays the good guy, and sometimes he plays the lawyer.

—MALCOLM FORD, son of actor Harrison Ford

The public lives with its lawyers in a love-hate relationship; the lawyer is both hero and villain. One lawyer who stalks the popular imagination is wise and kind, puffing his pipe while dispensing pearls of wisdom to the comfort of all. This lawyer relieves the distressed and is admired for his dignity, knowledge, skill, and dedication, not to mention his high social prestige. Another lawyer is pictured as a sorcerer, breaking contracts, and pulling legal rabbits from hats, on cue and with proper payment. He may be disputatious, rapacious, conniving, greedily sucking in fees, and thoroughly unprincipled—a hired gun.

—BERTRAM HARNETT
from *Law, Lawyers, and Laymen*

A man who never graduated from school might steal from a freight car. But a man who attends college and graduates as a lawyer might steal the whole railroad.

—THEODORE ROOSEVELT
to his son on becoming a lawyer

A lawyer is a man who helps you get what is coming to him.

—LAURENCE J. PETER, educator and writer

The first thing we do, let's kill all the lawyers.

—SHAKESPEARE from *Henry IV*

Anyone who believes a better day dawns when lawyers are eliminated bears the burden of explaining who will take their place. Who will protect the poor, the injured, the victims of negligence, the victims of racial discrimination and the victims of racial violence?

—JOHN J. CURTIN, JR., lawyer

⌘

When you start out in criminal law you envision yourself acting on behalf of innocent people accused of crime. You imagine a lifetime in Perry Mason Land, getting those wonderful innocent folks off.... What you mostly find—in the lower echelons of crime, at least—are losers, people who can't figure out much of anything. And so you fight for those people since no one else has. They're at the bottom of the barrel, most will never rise any higher, and as long as they're down there the bullies among us—who aren't all that clever, either—will keep slamming them.

—LESLIE ABRAMSON from *The Defense Is Ready*

Being a lawyer means not only sharing the pain of other people's suffering but also accepting the burden of their trust. In the final moment, being a lawyer isn't about winning or losing. It's about keeping faith.

—JOHNNIE L. COCHRAN, JR., from *Journey to Justice*

All About the Law

Law...begins when someone takes to doing something someone else does not like.

—KARL LLEWELLYN, lawyer, professor, and legal scholar

Pretty much all law consists in forbidding men to do some things that they want to do.

—OLIVER WENDELL HOLMES, JR., Supreme Court Justice

The precepts of the law are these: to live honestly, to injure no one, and to give everyone his due.

—Justinian I from the *Justinian Code*

Law is the witness and external deposit of our moral life. Its history is the history of the moral development of the race.

—Oliver Wendell Holmes, Jr.,
Supreme Court Justice

Fragile as reason is and limited as law is as the institutionalized medium of reason, that's all we have standing between us and the tyranny of mere will and the cruelty of unbridled, undisciplined feeling.

—Felix Frankfurter, Supreme Court Justice

Common sense often makes a good law.

    —WILLIAM O. DOUGLAS, Supreme Court Justice

The good of the people is the supreme law.

    —CICERO, Roman statesman

Any laws but those which men make for themselves are laughable.

    —RALPH WALDO EMERSON, essayist and poet

No written law has ever been more binding than unwritten custom supported by popular opinion.

    —CARRIE CHAPMAN CATT, reformer

The life of the law has not been logic; it has been experience.

—OLIVER WENDELL HOLMES, JR.,
Supreme Court Justice

Laws should be like clothes.
They should be made to fit the people they are
meant to serve.

—CLARENCE DARROW, lawyer and writer

If you like laws and sausages, you should never watch either one being made.

—OTTO VON BISMARCK, statesman and
first chancellor of German Empire

Laws, like houses, lean on one another.

—EDMUND BURKE, statesman and orator

The law, in its majestic equality, forbids all men to sleep under bridges, to beg in the streets, and to steal bread—the rich as well as the poor.

—ANATOLE FRANCE, writer

No man is above the law and no man is below it; nor do we ask any man's permission when we require him to obey it. Obedience to the law is demanded as a right, not asked as a favor.

—THEODORE ROOSEVELT,
26th president of the United States

I think that we should be men first, and subjects afterward. It is not desirable to cultivate a respect for the law, so much as for the right.

—HENRY DAVID THOREAU from *Civil Disobedience*

Our defense is not in armaments, nor in science, nor in going underground. Our defense is in law and order.

—ALBERT EINSTEIN, physicist

There is plenty of law at the end of a nightstick.

—Attributed to GROVER A. WHALEN

Law cannot persuade where it cannot punish.

—THOMAS FULLER, cleric

I fought the law and the law won.

—Sonny Curtis, "I Fought the Law,"
recorded by the Bobby Fuller Four

A great many people in this country are worried about law-and-order. And a great many people are worried about justice. But one thing is certain: You cannot have either until you have both.

—Ramsey Clark, U.S. attorney general

Laws too gentle are seldom obeyed;
too severe, seldom executed.

—Benjamin Franklin, statesman and philosopher

Ignorance of the law is no excuse, in any country. If it were, the laws would lose their effect, because it can be always pretended.

—THOMAS JEFFERSON,
3rd president of the United States

There is something monstrous in commands couched in invented and unfamiliar language; an alien master is the worst of all. The language of the law must not be foreign to the ears of those who are to obey it.

—LEARNED HAND from "Is There a Common Will"

Laws are like spiders' webs: If some poor weak creature come up against them, it is caught; but a big one can break through and get away.

—SOLON, Athenian statesman

The great can protect themselves, but the poor and humble require the arm and shield of the law.

—ANDREW JACKSON
in letter to John Quincy Adams

There is far too much law for those who can afford it and far too little for those who cannot.

—DEREK C. BOK from "A Flawed System"

Possession is nine-tenths of the law.

—WILLIAM MURRAY (first Earl of Mansfield), jurist

Laws and institutions are constantly tending to gravitate. Like clocks, they must be occasionally cleansed, and wound up, and set to true time.

—HENRY WARD BEECHER from *Life Thoughts*

I think there never was a people so choked and stultified by forms. We adore the forms of law, instead of making them vehicles of wisdom and justice.

—RALPH WALDO EMERSON, essayist and poet

Law must be stable and yet it cannot stand still.

—ROSCOE POUND from
Interpretations of Legal History

It usually takes 100 years to make a law, and then, after it has done its work, it usually takes 100 years to get rid of it.

—HENRY WARD BEECHER, cleric and writer

No people is shrewder than the American in perceiving when a law works ill, nor prompter in repealing it.

—JAMES BRYCE from *The American Commonwealth*

꧁꧂

The law is not a series of calculating machines where definitions and answers come tumbling out when the right levers are pushed.

—WILLIAM O. DOUGLAS, Supreme Court Justice

꧁꧂

Laws are a dead letter without courts to expound and define their true meaning and operation.

—ALEXANDER HAMILTON from *The Federalist*

꧁꧂

That is the beauty of the Common Law, it is a maze and not a motorway.

—LORD DIPLOCK, jurist

The Constitution was not made to fit us like a strait jacket. In its elasticity lies its chief greatness.

—WOODROW WILSON,
28th president of the United States

If an obscure Florida convict named Clarence Earl Gideon had not sat down in his prison cell with a pencil and paper to write a letter to the Supreme Court, and if the Court had not taken the trouble to look for merit in that one crude petition, among all the bundles of mail it must receive every day, the vast machinery of American Law would have gone on functioning undisturbed.

—ROBERT F. KENNEDY,
U.S. attorney general and politician

Our Constitution was not written in the sands to be washed away by each wave of new judges blown in by each successive political wind.

—HUGO L. BLACK, Supreme Court Justice

It is a fortunate thing for society that the courts do not get the same chance at the Ten Commandments as they do at the Constitution of the United States.

—PHILANDER C. JOHNSON from *Senator Sorghum's Primer of Politics*

A law can be both economic folly and constitutional.

—ANTONIN SCALIA, Supreme Court Justice

Any fool can make a rule.

—HENRY DAVID THOREAU, writer

Law is a majestic edifice, sheltering all of us, each stone of which rests on another.

—JOHN GALSWORTHY, writer and dramatist

An excess of law inescapably weakens the rule of law.

—Laurence H. Tribe, lawyer, professor, and writer

Those who are too lazy and comfortable to think for themselves and be their own judges obey the laws. Others sense their own laws within them.

—Hermann Hesse, writer

However harmless a thing is, if the law forbids it most people will think it wrong.

—W. Somerset Maugham, writer

Good men must not obey the laws too well.

—Ralph Waldo Emerson, essayist and poet

Damn the law! I want the [Panama] canal built.

—Attributed to THEODORE ROOSEVELT

Laws were made to be broken.

—CHRISTOPHER NORTH, poet, essayist, and critic

We should never forget that everything Hitler did in Germany was "legal" and everything the Hungarian freedom fighters did in Hungary was "illegal."

—MARTIN LUTHER KING, JR.
from "Letter from Birmingham City Jail"

If we desire respect for the law we must first make the law respectable.

—LOUIS D. BRANDEIS, Supreme Court Justice

I know no method to secure the repeal of bad or obnoxious laws so effective as their stringent execution.

—ULYSSES S. GRANT, from his inaugural address, March 4, 1869

One of the greatest delusions in the world is the hope that the evils in this world are to be cured by legislation.

—THOMAS BRACKETT REED, politician

It may be true that the law cannot make a man love me, but it can keep him from lynching me, and I think that's pretty important.

—MARTIN LUTHER KING JR., civil rights leader

If the law is upheld only by government officials, then all law is at an end.

—HERBERT HOOVER, in a message to Congress, 1929

Go to law for a sheep and lose your cow.

—GERMAN PROVERB

Law is a Bottomless Pit

—JOHN ARBUTHNOT,
17th-century physician and writer

The one great principle of the English law is, to make business for itself.

—CHARLES DICKENS from *Bleak House*

Conscience and law will never go together.

—WILLIAM CONGREVE from *The Double Dealer*

❦

The law sees and treats women the way men see and treat women.

—CATHARINE MACKINNON,
law professor, feminist, and writer

❦

Morality cannot be legislated, but behavior can be regulated. Judicial decrees may not change the heart, but they can restrain the heartless.

—MARTIN LUTHER KING, JR., from *Strength to Love*

❦

The best use of good laws is to teach men to trample bad laws under their feet.

—WENDELL PHILLIPS, reformer

It is the spirit and not the form of law that keeps justice alive.

—EARL WARREN, Supreme Court Justice

On The Practice of Law...

Law is quite overdone. It is fallen to the ground, and a man must have great powers to raise himself in it to either honor or profit. The mob of the profession gets as little money and less respect, than they would be digging the earth.

—THOMAS JEFFERSON
from *Writings of Thomas Jefferson*

Next to the confrontation between two highly trained, finely honed batteries of lawyers, jungle warfare is a stately minuet.

—BILL VEECK from *The Hustler's Handbook*

The value of a lawyer's services is not measured by time or labor merely. The practice of law is an art in which success depends as much as in any other art on the application of imagination—and sometimes inspiration—to the subject-matter.

—JOHN M. WOOLSEY from
Woodbury v. Andrew Jergens Co.

Whatever the commentators may say, a trial is not really a struggle between opposing lawyers but between opposing stories.

—JOHNNIE L. COCHRAN, JR., from *Journey To Justice*

Most of the great trial lawyers I know are very, very scared. Fear, for an actor, stirs you to a greater performance.

—ARTHUR LIMAN quoted in *What They Said in 1989*

His oral statement to be persuasive must at least be *clear*.... To clarity he must add *force*; for the court, if captured at all, must be taken by storm.

—ROBERT H. JACKSON, Supreme Court Justice

A high-profile trial imposes almost unimaginable stress and pressure. I discovered by accident that there is only one way to survive them unscathed: Never forget that you are there to represent your client's interests and for no other reason.

—JOHNNIE L. COCHRAN, JR., from *Journey To Justice*

The effective lawyer, like the .300 hitter, is one who, by a blend of common sense and a savvy grasp of human nature, knows when an adversary will try to overpower him and when he'll throw him a curveball.

—MARK H. MCCORMACK
from *The Terrible Truth About Lawyers*

Our wrangling lawyers...are so litigious and busy here on earth, that I think they will plead their clients' causes hereafter, some of them in hell.

—ROBERT BURTON
from *The Anatomy of Melancholy*

I used to say that, as Solicitor General, I made three arguments of every case. First came the one that I planned—as I thought, logical, coherent, complete. Second was the one actually presented—interrupted, incoherent, disjointed, disappointing. The third was the utterly devastating argument that I thought of after going to bed that night.

—ROBERT H. JACKSON from "Advocacy before the Supreme Court: Suggestions for Effective Case Presentations"

[Cross-examination] is beyond any doubt the greatest legal engine ever invented for the discovery of truth.... Cross-examination, not trial by jury, is the great and permanent contribution of the Anglo-American system of law to improved methods of trial-procedure.

—JOHN H. WIGMORE from *A Treatise on the System of Evidence in Trials at Common Law*

Never, never, never, on cross-examination ask a witness a question you don't already know the answer to, was a tenet I absorbed with my baby-food. Do it, and you'll often get an answer you don't want, an answer that might wreck your case.

—HARPER LEE from *To Kill a Mockingbird*

The art of cross-examination is not the art of examining crossly. It's the art of leading the witness through a line of propositions he agrees to until he's forced to agree to the *one fatal question.*

—CLIFFORD MORTIMER, lawyer and writer

In cross-examination, as in fishing, nothing is more ungainly than a fisherman pulled into the water by his catch.

—LOUIS NIZER, lawyer and writer

The terrible truth is that the longer a case goes on, the less it is worth, except to the lawyers.

—MARK H. MCCORMACK
from *The Terrible Truth About Lawyers*

I hate to see it. People waste precious years in court, harboring grudges, nursing old wounds, seeking revenge for real or imagined slights. Their lives are passing them by; they never get those years back. Becoming bitter over *bupkis* (nothing) is absurd.

JUDGE JUDY SHEINDLIN
from *Beauty Fades, Dumb is Forever*

Nearly every lawsuit is an insult to the intelligence of both plaintiff and defendant.

—EDGAR WATSON HOWE from *Sinner Sermons*

Everytime a lawyer writes something, he is not writing for posterity, he is writing so that endless others of his craft can make a living out of trying to figure out what he said, 'course perhaps he hadn't really said anything, that's what makes it hard to explain.

—WILL ROGERS, actor and humorist

It is as if the ordinary language we use every day has a hidden set of signals, a kind of secret code.

—WILLIAM STAFFORD, writer, professor, and poet

I abhor, loathe and despise these long discourses, and agree with Carducci the Italian poet who died some years ago that a man who takes half a page to say what can be said in a sentence will be damned.

—OLIVER WENDELL HOLMES, JR.,
Supreme Court Justice

Of course many summary-judgment motions are denied. I had a friend who clerked for a judge who had an "one-inch rule." If the briefs were thicker than an inch, he would deny summary judgment automatically. "There must be a disputed fact in there somewhere."

—THOMAS GEOGHEGAN from *In America's Court*

The aim of law is the maximum gratification of the nervous system of man.

—LEARNED HAND, jurist

And whether you're an honest man, or whether
    you're a thief,
Depends on whose solicitor has given me
    my brief.

—W. S. GILBERT, playwright

The screening process through which law firms choose new partners is perhaps as well considered as anything this side of a papal election.

—NEAL JOHNSTON, politician

Law [is] a horrible business.

—CLARENCE DARROW, lawyer and writer

Some lawyers never quite recover from the disillusionment that attends the first rude rush of actual practice, and they quickly take on a pragmatic cynicism that will help them flourish in our far-from-perfect system. Others resolve to keep their ideals intact and to battle the status quo even while being embroiled in it. And still others begin quickly to wonder if they really want to be practicing attorneys after all.

—MARK H. MCCORMACK
from *The Terrible Truth About Lawyers*

No one is under pressure. There wasn't a light on when I left at 2 o'clock this morning.

—HOYT MOONE, lawyer

Law practice is the exact opposite of sex: even when it's good, it's bad.

—MORTIMER ZUCKERMAN, publisher and lawyer

Judge and Jury

We must never forget that the only real source of power that we as judges can tap is the respect of the people.

—THURGOOD MARSHALL, Supreme Court Justice

No man is allowed to be a judge in his own cause because his interest would certainly bias his judgment and, not improbably, corrupt his integrity.

—JAMES MADISON from *The Federalist*

When a judge sits in judgment over a fellow man, he should feel as if a sword is pointed at his own heart.

—TALMUD

Law is what a judge dispenses. The judge, however, is no representative of the average man's common sense. A certain remoteness from the experiences of everyday life and a certain rigidity of viewpoint are essential to his role as judge

—GERHART HUSSERL, legal scholar

We must remember that we have to make judges out of men, and that by being made judges their prejudices are not diminished and their intelligence is not increased.

—ROBERT G. INGERSOLL, orator and writer

A judge is...surrounded by people who keep telling him what a wonderful fellow he is. And if he once begins to believe it, he is a lost soul.

—HAROLD R. MEDINA, jurist

I don't want to know what the law is, I want to know who the judge is.

—ROY COHN, lawyer

A judge is not supposed to know anything about the facts of life until they have been presented into evidence and explained to him at least three times.

—HUBERT LISTER PARKER,
British Lord Chief Justice

The acme of judicial distinction means the ability to look a lawyer straight in the eyes for two hours and not to hear a damned word he says.

—JOHN MARSHALL, Supreme Court Justice

Consider what you think justice requires, and decide accordingly. But never give your reasons; for your judgement will probably be right, but your reasons will certainly be wrong.

—WILLIAM MURRAY, British jurist,
giving advice to a newly appointed
colonial governor ignorant in the law

[On the sentencing of criminal defendants:] Here I am an old man in a long nightgown making muffled noises at people who may be no worse than I am.

—LEARNED HAND, jurist

[Packing the Supreme Court] can't be done.... I've tried it and it doesn't work. Whenever you put a man on the Supreme Court, he ceases to be your friend.

—HARRY S TRUMAN,
33rd president of the United States

Something about our courtroom scares lawyers to death. Some fellows have fainted.

—WILLIAM J. BRENNAN JR., Supreme Court Justice

A judge rarely performs his functions adequately unless the case before him is adequately presented.

—LOUIS D. BRANDEIS, Supreme Court Justice

The Court's opinion will accomplish the seemingly impossible feat of leaving this area of the law more confused than it found it.

—WILLIAM H. REHNQUIST, Supreme Court Justice,
in his dissenting opinion in *Roe v. Wade*

A good judge conceives quickly, judges slowly.

—GEORGE HERBERT, poet

We do not inquire what the legislature meant; we ask only what the statute means.

—OLIVER WENDELL HOLMES, JR.,
Supreme Court Justice

The judge answers questions of law; the jury answers questions of fact.

—LATIN SAYING

The hungry judges soon the sentence sign,
And wretches hang that jurymen may dine.

—ALEXANDER POPE, poet

Judges are the weakest link in our system of justice,
and they are also the most protected.

—ALAN DERSHOWITZ, lawyer and writer

It has been said that a judge is a member of the
Bar who once knew a Governor.

—CURTIS BOK from *The Backbone of the Herring*

A judge is a law student who marks his own
examination papers.

—H. L. MENCKEN, journalist and writer

The judge weighs the arguments and puts a brave face on the matter, and, since there must be a decision, decides as he can, and hopes he has done justice.

—Ralph Waldo Emerson, essayist and poet

A jury consists of twelve persons chosen to decide who has the better lawyer.

—Robert Frost, poet

Only lawyers and mental defectives are automatically exempt for jury duty.

—George Bernard Shaw, writer and dramatist

A jury too frequently have at least one member, more ready to hang the panel than to hang the traitor.

—ABRAHAM LINCOLN,
16th president of the United States

Percy Foremen and I once had an argument as to which of us had picked the most stupid jury. I think I won with one that returned a verdict which amounted to "Not guilty with a recommendation of clemency because of reasonable doubt."

—F. LEE BAILEY, lawyer

I never saw twelve men in my life, that, if you could get them to understand a human case, were not true and right.

—CLARANCE DARROW, lawyer and writer

I have what jurors want. They want charisma. They want a fight in the courtroom. They don't want placidity. They don't want a one-dimensional lawsuit. They came here for a show. And they want to do what's right.

—Philip Corboy, lawyer

It is the "ordinariness" of the jury that finally emerges as its unique strength.

—Melvyn B. Zerman, writer

Jury duty [is] a bog of quicksand on the path to justice.

—Sidney Bernard from "The Waiting Game"

We, the jury, find our client not guilty.

—VERDICT OF A JURY IN THE MUNICIPAL COURT
AT FORT SMITH, ARKANSAS,
in a drunkenness case, December 2, 1933

A fox should not be of the jury at a goose's trial.

—THOMAS FULLER, cleric

I would rather have my fate in the hands of 23 representative citizens of the county than in the hands of a politically appointed judge.

—ROBERT MORGENTHAU,
New York City District Attorney defending the
secrecy of grand jury proceedings

And Justice
For All

Justice is indiscriminately due to all, without regard to numbers, wealth, or rank.

—JOHN JAY, Supreme Court Justice

The Court's authority—possessed of neither the purse nor the sword—ultimately rests on substantial public confidence in its moral sanctions.

—FELIX FRANKFURTER, Supreme Court Justice

Judging from the main portions of the history of the world, so far, justice is always in jeopardy.

—WALT WHITMAN from *Democratic Vistas*

Man's capacity for justice makes democracy possible, but man's inclination to injustice makes democracy necessary.

—REINHOLD NIEBUHR from *The Children of Light and the Children of Darkness*

The whole history of the world is summed up in the fact that, when nations are strong, they are not always just, and when they wish to be just, they are no longer strong.

—WINSTON CHURCHILL, statesman and writer

Justice, though due to the accused, is due to the accuser also. The concept of fairness must not be strained till it is narrowed to a filament. We are to keep the balance true.

—Benjamin N. Cardozo, Supreme Court Justice

In America, an acquittal doesn't mean you're innocent, it means you beat the rap. My clients lose even when they win.

—F. Lee Bailey, lawyer

The sword of the law should never fall but on those whose guilt is so apparent as to be pronounced by their friends as well as foes.

—Thomas Jefferson,
3rd president of the United States

Justice is truth in action.

—JOSEPH JOUBERT, ethicist and essayist

There is in this country no superior, dominant, ruling class of citizens. There is no caste here. Our Constitution is color-blind, and neither knows nor tolerates classes among citizens. In respect of civil rights, all citizens are equal before the law.

—JOHN MARSHALL HARLAN, in a dissenting Supreme Court opinion in *Plessy v. Ferguson,* 1896

When a just cause reaches its flood tide...whatever stands in the way must fall before its overwhelming power.

—CARRIE CHAPMAN CATT, reformer

There may be times when we are powerless to prevent injustice, but there must never be a time when we fail to protest.

—ELIE WIESEL, writer

The success of any legal system is measured by its fidelity to the universal ideal of justice.

—EARL WARREN, Supreme Court Justice

This is a court of law, young man, not a court of justice.

—OLIVER WENDELL HOLMES, JR.,
Supreme Court Justice

Injustice is relatively easy to bear; what stings is justice.

—H. L. MENCKEN, journalist and writer

Justice delayed is justice denied.

—PROVERB

There is no such thing as justice—in or out of court.

—CLARENCE DARROW, lawyer and writer

For justice, though she's painted blind,
Is to the weaker side inclined.

—SAMUEL BUTLER, writer

Justice may be blind, but she has very sophisticated listening devices.

—EDGAR ARGO from *Funny Times*

In England, justice is open to all—like the Ritz Hotel.

—Anonymous

Justice without force is impotent; force without justice is tyranny.

—Pascal, scientist and philosopher

All justice comes from God—he alone is its source.

—Jean Jacques Rousseau from *The Social Contract*

Injustice anywhere is a threat to justice everywhere.

—Martin Luther King Jr., civil rights leader

The Paper Chase

Look well to the right of you, look well to the left of you, for one of you three won't be here next year.

—SAYING heard by 1st-year law students everywhere

If law school is so hard to get through, how come there are so many lawyers?

—CALVIN TRILLIN, writer and humorist

I will tell you honestly that I am sick at heart of this place [Harvard Law School] and almost everything connected with it. I know not what the temple of the law may be to those who have entered it, but to me it seems very cold and cheerless about the threshold.

—OLIVER WENDELL HOLMES, SR.,
physician, professor, and writer

Make no mistake, terror is an integral part of the law school experience, and the long-term consequence of that terror is to make it very difficult for lawyers to admit when they've made an error or when they simply don't know something. The ultimate sin is being at a loss for words.

—MARK H. MCCORMACK
from *The Terrible Truth About Lawyers*

I had studied law an entire week, and then given it up because it was so prosy and tiresome.

—MARK TWAIN from *Roughing It*

The study of the law is useful in a variety of points of view. It qualifies a man to be useful to himself, to his neighbors and to the public. It is the most certain stepping-stone to preferment in the political line.

—THOMAS JEFFERSON,
3rd president of the United States

The mode is very simple, though laborious and tedious. It is only to get the books and read and study them carefully.... Work, work, work is the main thing.

—ABRAHAM LINCOLN,
16th president of the United States

Law school taught me one thing: how to take two situations that are exactly the same and show how they are different.

—Hart Pomerantz, lawyer

Law school has been described as a place for the accumulation of learning. First-year students bring some in; third-year students take none away. Hence it accumulates.

—Daniel R. White
from *The Official Lawyer's Handbook*

There is always room at the top.

—Daniel Webster's reply when told not to become a lawyer because the profession was overcrowded.

All of us were learning to think like lawyers—but not to be lawyers.... At UCLA, in the fall of 1966 when I arrived and for many years after, nobody learned anything about the actual practice of law. What we learned was the foundation on which the edifice of rules and rights and sanctions was built. The notion was that if you understood the reasons for the rules, you could analyze problems and fashion solutions that reflected society's values even if you didn't know the actual rules (the letter of the law). For the kind of insecure student who needed to know "the answer," law school was a nerve-racking three years.

—LESLIE ABRAMSON from *The Defense Is Ready*

If the weakness of the apprentice system was to produce advocates without scholarship, the weakness of the law school system is to turn out scholars with no skill at advocacy.

—ROBERT H. JACKSON
from "Training the Trial Lawyer"

I got into Harvard and I got into Yale, and actually I went to a cocktail reception at the Harvard Law School with a young man who was, I think, a second-year Harvard law student. And he introduced me to one of the legendary Harvard law professors by saying, 'Professor So-and-so, this is Hillary Rodham. She's trying to decide between us and our nearest competitor.' And this man, with his three-piece suit and his bow tie, looked at me and said, 'First of all, we have no nearest competitor, and, secondly, we don't need any more women.' And that's how I decided to go to Yale.

—HILLARY RODHAM CLINTON,
U.S. senator and former first lady

Lawyers' Wisdom

The leading rule for the lawyer, as for the man of every other calling, is diligence. Leave nothing for to-morrow which can be done to-day. Never let your correspondence fall behind.

—ABRAHAM LINCOLN
from "Notes for a Law Lecture"

A lawyer has no business with the justice or injustice of the cause which he undertakes, unless his client asks his opinion, and then he is bound to give it honestly. The justice or injustice of the cause is to be decided by the judge.

—SAMUEL JOHNSON, writer and critic

Discourage litigation. Persuade your neighbors to compromise whenever you can. Point out to them how the nominal winner is often a *real* loser–in fees, and expenses, and waste of time. As a peacemaker the lawyer has a superior opertunity [sic] of being a good man. There will still be business enough.

—ABRAHAM LINCOLN
from "Notes on the Practice of Law"

Agree, for the Law is costly.

—JOHN CLARK, Supreme Court Justice

Praise the adversary. He is the catalyst by which you bill your client. Damn the client. He is your true enemy.

—STEVEN J. KUMBLE, lawyer

[The ideal client is] the very wealthy man in very great trouble.

—JOHN STERLING, lawyer

As in law so in war, the longest purse finally wins.

—MOHANDAS K. GANDHI, spiritual leader

[A lawyer] can never excuse himself for accepting a defendant's confidence and then betraying it by a half-hearted defense.

—EDWARD BENNETT WILLIAMS
from *One Man's Freedom*

What allows skilled lawyers—and can allow all of us—to function well under great duress is *the ability to strike a balance between commitment and detachment.*

—MARK H. MCCORMACK
from *The Terrible Truth About Lawyers*

If there were no bad people there would be no good lawyers.

—CHARLES DICKENS, novelist

It is better that ten guilty persons escape than one innocent suffer.

—WILLIAM BLACKSTONE
from *Commentaries on the Laws of England*

We must look away from the piecemeal law books, the miscellaneous and disconnected statutes and legal maxims, the court decisions, to the life of men.

—WOODROW WILSON from "The Law and the Facts"

In law it is good policy never to *plead* what you *need* not, lest you oblige yourself to *prove* what you *can* not.

—ABRAHAM LINCOLN,
16th president of the United States

Everything is negotiable—though this is one of the things that lawyers would just as soon not have clients realize.

—MARK H. MCCORMACK
from *The Terrible Truth About Lawyers*

Facts are stubborn things; and whatever may be our wishes, our inclinations, or the dictates of our passions, they cannot alter the state of facts and evidence.

—JOHN ADAMS, arguing in defense of the British soldiers involved in the Boston Massacre, December, 1770

A verbal contract isn't worth the paper it is written on.

—SAM GOLDWYN, motion-picture producer

No weight whatever to confessions outside the courtroom!

—ANONYMOUS

If you stand on principle, you cannot lose. Because even if you lose, you still have your principles.

—Janet Reno, U.S. attorney general

Every skilled person is to be believed with reference to his own art.

—Legal maxim

The burden of proof lies upon him who affirms, not upon him who denies.

—Latin saying

When you have no basis for an argument, abuse the plaintiff.

—Cicero, Roman orator and statesman

When the law is against you, argue the facts. When the facts are against you, argue the law. When both are against you, call the other lawyer names.

—Lawyer's Rule quoted by Paul Dickson, writer

It is always wise, as it is also fair, to test a man by the standards of his own day, and not by those of another.

—Odell Shepard, poet

Only painters and lawyers can change white to black.

—Proverb

One lawyer makes work for another

—Spanish saying

Where there is consent, there is no injury.

—S<small>PANISH SAYING</small>

Resolve to be honest at all events: and if in your judgment you cannot be an honest lawyer, resolve to be honest without being a lawyer. Choose some other occupation.

—A<small>BRAHAM</small> L<small>INCOLN</small>,
16th president of the United States

Legal Wit

An Irishman stopped before a grave in a cemetery, containing the tombstone declaring: "Here lies a lawyer and an honest man."

"An' who'd ever think," he murmured, "there'd be room for two men in that one little grave!"

–from THE WORLD'S BEST JOKES
edited by Lewis Copeland

Lawyers should not marry other lawyers. This is called inbreeding, from which comes idiot children and other lawyers.

–DAVID WAYNE from *Adam's Rib*

He reminds me of the man who murdered both his parents, and then, when sentence was about to be pronounced, pleaded for mercy on the grounds that he was an orphan.

—Attributed to ABRAHAM LINCOLN

A lawyer's dream of heaven—every man reclaimed his property at the resurrection, and each tried to recover it from all his forefathers.

—SAMUEL BUTLER, writer

Lawyer, *n.* One skilled in circumvention of the law.
—AMBROSE BIERCE from *The Devil's Dictionary*

Litigant, *n.* A person about to give up his skin for the hope of retaining his bones.
—AMBROSE BIERCE from *The Devil's Dictionary*

Litigation, *n.* A machine which you go into as a pig and come out of as a sausage.

—AMBROSE BIERCE from *The Devil's Dictionary*

The only thing a lawyer won't question is the legitimacy of his mother.

—W. C. FIELDS, entertainer

When the thirty-year-old lawyer died he said to St. Peter, "How can you do this to me? —a heart attack at my age? I'm only thirty."

Replied St. Peter: "When we looked at your total hours billed we figured you were ninety-five."

—ANONYMOUS

Why don't sharks eat lawyers? Professional courtesy.

—ANONYMOUS

A lawyer with his briefcase can steal more than a hundred men with guns.

—MARIO PUZO from *The Godfather*

This trial is a travesty; it's a travesty of a mockery of a sham of a mockery of a travesty of two mockeries of a sham. I move for a mistrial.

—WOODY ALLEN from *Bananas*

A man may as well open an oyster without a knife as a lawyer's mouth without a fee.

—BARTEN HOLIDAY, cleric and writer

How can you tell if a lawyer is lying?
His lips are moving.

—A<small>NONYMOUS</small>

A solicitor is a man who calls in a person he doesn't know to sign a contract he hasn't seen to buy property he doesn't want with money he hasn't got.

—S<small>IR</small> D<small>INGWALL</small> B<small>ATESON</small>, lawyer

Bluster, sputter, question, cavil; but be sure your argument is intricate enough to confound the court.

—W<small>ILLIAM</small> W<small>YCHERLEY</small>, dramatist

A potential client asked his lawyer what he would charge for taking on a particular case.

After considering the merits of the case, the lawyer answered that he would take it on for a contingency fee.

"What is a contingency fee?" asked the client.

The lawyer smiled. "A contingency fee means that if I don't win your suit, I don't get anything. If I do win your suit, you don't get anything."

—SID BEHRMAN, comedian

"I told you you should've got yourself some legal advice before running to a lawyer." (overheard in a courthouse corridor).

—*THE NEW YORKER*

Upon seeing an elderly lady for the drafting of her will, the attorney charged her $100. She gave him a $100 bill, not noticing that stuck to it was a second $100 bill. Immediately the ethical question arose in the attorney's mind: "Do I tell my partner?"

—MICHAEL RAFFERTY from *Skid Marks*

You have a pretty good case, Mr. Pitkin. How much justice can you afford?

—*NEW YORKER* cartoon

It was so cold one day last February that I saw a lawyer with his hands in his own pockets.

—ROBERT PETERSON, comedian